THE WATER THAT CAUGHT ON FIRE

1 KINGS 17–18 FOR CHILDREN

Written by Joann Scheck

Illustrated by Bob Fanter

Concordia Publishing House

ARCH Books

A long time ago
King Ahab was wed
to a wife who was wicked.
One day the queen said,

"Why do we worship
a God we can't see?
Just think how exciting
a stone god would be!"

So the king built a temple to please his new bride.

And they knelt down to Baal at an altar inside.

Elijah, God's prophet,
then came to the king.
"Get rid of this temple.
Get rid of this thing.
He's not the true God,
this one you call Baal.
Come worship the Lord!
He'll show you He's real.
For three years He'll hold back
the rain from the sky.
The clouds will be empty;
the plants will all die."

And just as he promised,
God stopped all the rain
till the fields full of wheat
and the fields full of grain,
the fruit on the trees
and the plants on the ground,
everything dried up
for miles all around.

But God told Elijah
to go to a spring
where he could drink water
and hide from the king.
The birds brought him bread,
and the birds brought him meat.
For three years Elijah
had plenty to eat.

The prophet came back then
to Ahab once more,
who still had his Baal
and prayed as before.

"O Ahab!" Elijah
cried out to the king.
"God kept back the rain;
He can do anything.
But since you insist
your god Baal is so strong,
come up to Mount Carmel.
I'll show you you're wrong."

From all over the kingdom
the people were called.
"Come up to Mount Carmel
next week," they were told.

They climbed up the hill
very early one day.
The king and his hundreds
of priests led the way.

At the top stood Elijah.
He called, "Priests of Baal,
we'll see who's a fake,
and we'll see who is real.
We'll each build an altar
on top of this hill.
Can your Baal burn it?
I know my God will."

Baal's four hundred fifty priests
brought stacks of wood
and built a big altar
as fast as they could.
They danced around it,
they started to pray
to Baal to send down
some fire right away.

Though they prayed the whole morning,
the wood was still there
when the priests looked around
at the end of their prayer.

Elijah called out to the priests,
"Look! It's noon!
Don't you think your old Baal
should answer you soon?
Pray louder and louder,
for maybe he's talking.
Or could he be sleeping?
Perhaps he's out walking."

The priests prayed and shouted;
they danced and they hopped.
By evening they all were
so tired they dropped.

Elijah stood up and said,
"Now it's my turn.
But wood is too easy
for my God to burn."
For his altar he piled
twelve big stones on the ground
and dug a deep trench
in a circle around.

"Oh, wait," said Elijah,
"we're not ready yet.
It still is too easy.
The wood must be wet!
Fill four jars with water,
and wet down the wood."
They made the whole altar
as wet as they could.
Elijah just smiled
and said to the men,
"Fill more jars with water,
and do it again."
Three times they brought water;
three times they did pour.
They poured it and poured it,
then poured it some more.
It splashed off the altar
and sloshed on the ground.
It filled up the trench
like a river around.

"And now," said Elijah,
"O Lord, I do pray,
Please burn up this altar
with fire right away."

Then suddenly out of the sky
roared a flame
that disappeared quickly
as fast as it came.
It burned up the wood
and the stones in a gust;
it dried up the water
and licked up the dust.

The people were quiet;
no one made a sound.
They fell on their faces
and knelt on the ground.

"From now on," they promised,
"we'll worship and praise
the Lord God of heaven
the rest of our days."

As the people went back
to their homes late that day,
Elijah stayed high
on the hilltop to pray.

While he knelt on the ground
with his head on his knees,
a little white cloud
rose up out of the seas.

So after three years
God at last sent the rain
till the fields full of wheat
and the fields full of grain,
the fruit on the trees
and the plants on the ground,
everything grew
in the land all around.

Dear Parents:

"Ahab did more to provoke the Lord, the God of Israel, to anger than all the kings of Israel who were before him," says the writer in 1 Kings 16:33. He and Queen Jezebel built an altar and a temple for Baal and led the people away from the true God to worship a man-made idol of stone.

Elijah brought the Word of the Lord to King Ahab, but he would not listen. Even three years without rain did not lead the king to repent.

But God did not reject His people. He took care of Elijah near a little stream and sent ravens to feed him. At the right time God sent Elijah back to Ahab, but he still turned away from God and prayed to Baal.

Through the word and action of Elijah God reached out to help His people. In answer to Elijah's prayer God sent fire to burn the wood and the stone of the altar. Even the water caught on fire. The people realized that the God of Elijah was true and that Baal, the god of Ahab, was false. The people repented and learned to trust in God again.

As a parent, you have the best opportunity to help your child recognize the false gods and idols today. You can lead him to trust in God, who is faithful to His promises, gives us all that we need, and above all, gives us His Son, Jesus Christ.

The Editor